P9-DGQ-877

# BEFORE WE EAT
## from farm to table

Pat Brisson    Illustrated by Mary Azarian

TILBURY HOUSE, PULISHERS · THOMASTON, MAINE

As we sit around this table
let's give thanks as we are able

to all the folks we'll never meet
who helped provide this food we eat.

They plowed the ground

and planted seeds,

tended fields,

removed the weeds.

They picked the food at harvest time,

working in the heat and grime.

They grazed the cattle,

fed the sows,

gathered eggs,

and milked the cows.

They fished from boats

out on the seas;

raised wheat

and nuts and honeybees.

Thank the ones who packed the crates,

sorted boxes, checked the weights.

Thank the drivers on the roads

in their trucks with heavy loads.

And all the clerks at all the stores

who did the grocery-selling chores.

Thank the ones who bought this food,

the ones who teach me gratitude.

Sitting at this meal we share,
we are grateful and aware,

sending thanks upon the air . . .

to those workers everywhere.

TILBURY HOUSE, PUBLISHERS
12 Starr Street, Thomaston, Maine 04861
800-482-1899 · www.tilburyhouse.com

First hardcover edition: May 15, 2014 · 10 9 8 7 6 5 4 3 2 1
ISBN 978-0-88448-352-6

For my grandchildren: Azalea, Pender, Eamon, Abigail and Mia —PB

With utmost respect for small farmers everywhere on Earth—stewards of the land, heart of community.  —MA

Library of Congress Cataloging-in-Publication Data

OCI 1 4 2014

Brisson, Pat.
Before we eat : from farm to table / Pat Brisson ; illustrated by Mary Azarian. — First hardcover edition.
    pages cm
Summary: As a family sits down to enjoy a meal, thoughts of those who provide the food, from farmers who plant and tend seeds to store clerks who sell groceries, fill each one with gratitude.
ISBN 978-0-88448-352-6 (hardcover : alk. paper)
[1. Stories in rhyme. 2. Gratitude—Fiction. 3. Food—Fiction.]  I. Azarian, Mary, illustrator. II. Title.
PZ8.3.B7745Bf 2014
[E]—dc23                        2013040076


Designed by Geraldine Millham, Westport, Massachusetts.
Printed and bound by Pacom Korea, Inc., Dang Jung-Dong 242-2, GungPo-si, Kyunggi-do, Korea; 2014.